Original title:
Shimmering Tropical Nights

Copyright © 2025 Creative Arts Management OÜ
All rights reserved.

Author: Alec Davenport
ISBN HARDBACK: 978-1-80581-690-4
ISBN PAPERBACK: 978-1-80581-217-3
ISBN EBOOK: 978-1-80581-690-4

Nectar of Fruit-laden Dreams

On the beach, a watermelon roll,
Laughter echoes, taking its toll.
Coconuts fall, like clumsy drunks,
Banana peels hide all the fun prunks.

Mango juice spills, sticky delight,
Dancing with passion, oh what a sight!
A pineapple hat spins on my head,
While papaya whispers, 'Go back to bed!'

Crickets Serenade the Tropical Twilight

Crickets chirp their evening tune,
While fireflies flicker, small as a spoon.
A lizard lounges, posing so grand,
Counting the stars as they form a band.

The moon makes jokes about the sun,
While bonfire sparks dance, having some fun.
Palm trees sway, not caring a bit,
As a coconut rolls and almost hits!

Beneath the Spangled Veil of Night

Beneath the stars, we trip and sway,
Grasshoppers join with their wild ballet.
A hammock strung between two trees,
Is where I nap, with a slight breeze.

An iguana grins with a toothy smile,
While we ponder each tropical style.
Laughter erupts over spilled drinks,
Even the seashells nod as one thinks.

A Tapestry of Aromas and Sounds

The scent of fried plantains fills the air,
While parrots gossip without a care.
A fragrant breeze carries tales of delight,
As laughter rides the waves into the night.

The tambourine shimmies below the stars,
While someone tries to dance with the jars.
Salsa spills, the rhythm is wild,
Even the fish in the sea seem beguiled.

Tranquil Murmurs of a Nightly Ocean

The waves, they giggle like a child,
As moonbeams dance, oh so wild.
Fish in sunglasses swim by,
Sipping sea-juice, oh my, oh my!

Crabs in top hats tap their feet,
To the rhythm of the ocean's beat.
Starfish come out to play the flute,
While jellyfish bounce in their cute suit!

The Heartbeat of an Island Dream

Palm trees sway, they tell a joke,
As coconuts fall with a gentle poke.
A parrot squawks, "Where's my drink?"
While iguanas join, in sync they wink.

The sandman slips on a banana peel,
And all the crabs just squeal and squeal.
Dancing dancers with coconut crowns,
Laugh as they twirl in their grass skirts' gowns.

Glow of Fireflies in the Night's Embrace

Fireflies twinkle, a disco ball,
As frogs in tuxedos start to crawl.
They croak a tune, oh what a sound,
While lightning bugs bounce all around!

A turtle wearing glasses, quite absurd,
Balances a drink, it's truly unheard!
The moon, a grin on its big, round face,
Looks down, chuckling at this wild place.

Tropical Rain's Whispered Secrets

Raindrops tap dance on the roof,
While ducks quack jokes that'll make you hoof.
Pineapples roll in a playful spree,
As umbrella mushrooms join for glee.

A snail in a raincoat begins to glide,
Across puddles, it cannot hide.
The laughter of the night goes on,
With playful spirits till the dawn.

Radiant Nights and Coconut Moonbeams

Under the glow of a big, round fruit,
Cats dance around, in tiny, high boots.
Laughter bounces off the palm tree leaves,
While parrots gossip in colorful weaves.

A watermelon falls, hitting my head,
I laugh so hard, I forget what I said.
Bananas swing down, like they're singin' a tune,
As I try to juggle, I'll soon be a cartoon!

Breeze-Kissed Blossoms in the Evening Glow

The flowers are giggling, look at them sway,
They dance like they're all going to Broadway.
Bees buzzing loudly, like they own the place,
Try to convince them to join a slow race.

A pineapple slips, causing quite the ruckus,
I watch it roll by and think it's just luck, us.
Mangoes fly high, like they're chasing the moon,
As I duck and chuckle, who knew fruit could swoon?

Velvet Skies Spattered with Dreams

Stars are all winking, I swear they know me,
One even whispered, "You're looking quite free!"
Clouds gathered 'round, thinking they're all the rage,
Yet here I am, acting like a singer on stage.

A comet zooms by with a silly old face,
I nearly fall over, it sets quite the pace.
The moon starts to giggle and winks with delight,
It's a cosmic joke on this magical night!

Enchanted Evenings Beneath the Banyan Tree

The banyan tree whispers stories galore,
I sit with my friends, we're ready for more.
The shadows are stretching, having a good time,
While fireflies twinkle with beats that can rhyme.

A lizard jumps by, says 'What's all the fuss?'
I toss him a chip, and he joins in the bus.
Our laughter rings loud, like a carnival's cheer,
As we share silly tales beneath branches near.

Pockets of Light in the Darkness

Stars bounce like frogs on a lake,
A disco ball fell from a great mistake.
The moon's wearing shades, looking quite sly,
While crickets tune up with a wink of an eye.

Fireflies dance in a wild conga line,
Leading the way with a searchlight shine.
A coconut laughs, rolling with glee,
As waves come to tickle, oh-so-playfully.

The palm trees sway in quite a jig,
Whispers of humor, oh so big!
A parrot in shades, squawking a tune,
Claims he's the king of the bright, round moon.

Cocktails in hand, the fruit is on fire,
Mangoes and laughter feed the desire.
Beneath all the giggles, the night takes a flight,
These pockets of fun keep the dark ever bright.

Nights Embroidery on the Sea's Surface

The ocean's a canvas with splashes of glee,
As dolphins embroider, happy and free.
Stars stitch their patterns with threads of light,
Making the waves giggle, what a delight!

A fish in a tuxedo does the cha-cha,
Underwater limbo like a quirky gala.
Seagulls join in with a caw and a spin,
Each flap and each flutter brings laughter within.

Sandy toes tangle in a messy retreat,
As beach balls bubble up, what a treat!
A crab on its shell gives a wink, don't you see?
While the tide plays tag like it's wild and spree.

With coconut drinks, we toast the night's cheer,
Calling all stars, bringing them near.
Under this blanket of silliness bright,
The evening unfolds like a comical flight.

Shimmering Dreams Beneath the Night Sky

Underneath the moon's bright glow,
Fish are wearing hats, you know!
Coconuts with smiles so wide,
Dance around like they just fried.

Crickets chirp their silly tunes,
While turtles try to croon like loons.
Palm trees sway in groovy style,
While flamingos jog and smile.

Starlit waves begin to splash,
Seagulls race without a crash.
Octopus playing chess with snails,
While laughter weaves through funny tales.

A hammock sways, it calls my name,
I join the fun, it's quite the game.
And all the critters sing and play,
Beneath the night, we laugh away.

Ethereal Whispers in the Island Breeze

Breezes tickle all the palms,
While monkeys boast their silly charms.
Crispy chips float past a clam,
As if it's all a tasty scam.

Lemonade served with a grin,
The parrots join, it's a win-win.
Sandcastles tip their hats in pride,
As hermit crabs go for a ride.

Jellyfish wear disco lights,
As frogs take turns to hold the kites.
The night is young, the laughter flows,
With every joke, the humor grows.

The stars are winking, what a sight!
As everyone dances with delight.
In this paradise of fun, we dare,
To laugh until we just can't bear.

A Tidal Dance Through Enchanted Dreams

Waves are twirling in a dance,
While crabs pull off a daring prance.
Starfish float on dreamlike beams,
As dolphins share the silliest themes.

Seashells gossip, oh so bold,
While seaweed whispers tales of old.
A turtle in a tutu spins,
While jellybeans replace our sins.

Manta rays wear shoes and twirl,
While all the fish around them whirl.
The ocean shimmies, full of cheer,
And laughter rings from ear to ear.

As we dive deep to swim and glide,
We join the fun like we're allied.
With every splash, we lose our care,
In this dreamland, joy is rare.

Echoes of Laughter at Dusk's Flare

As the sun bows with a wink,
Crabs and crickets start to clink.
Coconuts shake off the sand,
And join the party, oh so grand!

Dusk descends with a quirky grin,
While fireflies start to spin.
A parrot jokes about a snake,
As silly pranks make the night break.

Turtles tell the silliest jokes,
While all the fish wear laughing cloaks.
The dusk is filled with cheerful yells,
Where humor weaves its magic spells.

Then as shadows start to blend,
We find ourselves around the bend.
With echoes of laughter everywhere,
In this night breeze, we're beyond compare.

Folklore of the Island's Heart

The coconut fell with a thud, oh dear,
A storyteller whispered, let's all gather near.
The crabs in tuxedos, they waltz on the sand,
And the fish swim by, dressed up, hand in hand.

The parrot squawks tales, colorful and bright,
Of a lost flip-flop that danced in the night.
The locals all giggle as they spin their yarns,
While the moon peeks out from behind swaying palms.

With laughter that bounces off ocean waves' roar,
They spin tales of giant sea slugs on the shore.
All the plants start to chuckle, so lively and spry,
Even the old sea turtles are rolling on by.

In the heart of the island, the stories take flight,
Making giggles and gaggles until morning light.
So come join the fun, leave your worries at bay,
With folklore and laughter, let's dance through the day.

Lullabies of the Gentle Sea

The sea sings a tune, soft as a cat,
While fish dabble dancing in old sailor's hat.
A jellyfish bounced, like a balloon on a string,
And the waves join in, oh the joy that they bring.

Sea turtles are snoring, just under the tide,
While crabs play chess, taking each other's side.
A starfish boasts tales of the ocean so deep,
As the sea cucumbers giggle and sleep.

The conch shells hum lullabies sweet and low,
But the seagulls squawk loudly, wanting a show.
The sand seems to wiggle, with creatures so spry,
As the sun takes a bow, saying, "Goodbye!"

With shells as our pillows, we drift off to dreams,
Where the moonlight collects all the sun's golden beams.
So hush now, little ones, let the sea sing along,
With laughter and soft waves, it's our favorite song.

Candles Flicker in the Warmth of Night

The candles are dancing, flicker and sway,
As the crickets join in on a night-time ballet.
A bowl of ripe bananas rolls under the table,
While the mango tree jiggles, oh so unstable.

The night breeze whispers secrets, oh so slight,
While the fireflies laugh, glowing with delight.
The rude gecko croaks, claiming he's the king,
While a raccoon shows off with a little bling.

With laughter so hearty, we toast marshmallow treats,
But the chocolate melts fast—what a sticky feat!
The ocean joins in, with a splash and a cheer,
As the stars hold a party, shining bright and clear.

So let's make a wish, and blow candles away,
With funny old stories, we'll stretch out our stay.
As the moon casts its glow on this magical plight,
And the world spins around in the warmth of the night.

Hidden Trails Beneath the Moonlight

The path to adventure is twinkling tonight,
As we chase after shadows, full of delight.
The crabs hold a concert, tapping their claws,
While the owls hoot loudly, giving raucous applause.

With flip-flops and giggles, we wander the shore,
While the clams sing us songs, oh just one encore!
The trails weave like ribbons, where mischief does lie,
And the moon snickers softly as the bats fly by.

A raccoon with sunglasses sips coconut drinks,
The seashells all gossip as the sly octopus winks.
Overhead, the stars seem to giggle and cheer,
As we stumble through grass with not much to fear.

So follow the laughter, let your heart take flight,
Through the hidden trails glowing in silver light.
With every small step, let the fun intertwine,
In this whimsical dance where the moon seems to shine.

Echoing Laughter Amongst the Palm Fronds

The coconuts begin to sway,
As monkeys dance and play.
They steal the drinks, oh what a sight,
While sunburnt tourists laugh with delight.

A crab in shades walks with flair,
Trying to impress the beachy air.
Seagulls squawk and join the fun,
Chasing flip-flops as they run.

A sandcastle stands proud and tall,
Till a wave crashes, it's a brawl!
With splashes, laughter fills the night,
As kids scream in pure delight.

The moon peeks down with a grin,
While lost flip-flops spin and spin.
Amongst the fronds, joy does ignite,
In this crazy, tropical night.

Windswept Dreams on Sangria Shores

The breeze brings tales with a twist,
Where every drink could not be missed.
Flip-flops flying through the air,
As sandcastles vanish without a care.

A parrot's squawk, a comedic scene,
As tourists dance like they've never been keen.
With drinks in hand, they lose their way,
Stumbling over the sun-kissed bay.

The beach ball bounces with a cheer,
While a dog tries to join in with beer.
In hilarious chaos, friends unite,
Laughing and sipping through the night.

Under starry skies, the antics flow,
As beach games take a funny show.
With giggles that echo across the shore,
Who knew tropical nights could mean so much more?

Mysteries Unfold in the Silver Light

A crab wearing shades starts to plot,
Sneaking snacks when he thinks it's hot.
As shadows dance, giggles abound,
In the moon's light, oddities are found.

There's a snorkeler chasing a fish,
While shouting their own silly wish.
A clever dolphin joins the fun,
With underwater jokes that weigh a ton.

Beach umbrellas twist in the breeze,
As kite surfers try to seize.
Onlookers laugh at comedic spills,
While sipping cocktails from quirky spills.

As the night wears on, secrets reveal,
A dancing starfish may just steal.
With all this laughter, oh what a sight,
Tonight's truths dance in silver light.

Embrace of the Sea in Gentle Caress

The waves whisper tales while they roll,
Between the giggles that take a toll.
Beach towels dance like they're in a race,
Chasing each other in the salty space.

Kids dig holes like there's treasure beneath,
While seaweed wraps like a funky wreath.
In laughter, they find a new disguise,
As crabs applaud with beady eyes.

Wind-chimes clatter in the soft sand,
As beachgoers craft a humorous band.
With each splash and slippery slide,
They share joy like a rising tide.

As the night deepens, stories are spun,
Under the glow of stars, oh what fun!
The sea holds secrets, calm and blessed,
In this carefree moment, we're truly dressed.

Celestial Waves of Moonlit Laughter

Beneath the stars, the crabs do dance,
With little top hats, they prance and prance.
A parrot squawks a joke so sly,
While fish below just roll and sigh.

Coconuts play hide and seek,
As monkeys swing, they start to peek.
The sea turtles laugh, 'Just take a break!'
As waves tickle toes, a chance to shake.

A dolphin flips with flair so neat,
While lounging sunburned on their seat.
The beach ball jumps, it starts to giggle,
And all the seashells join in the wiggle.

With laughter echoing through the night,
Each heart feels light, it's pure delight.
So grab a friend, let's toast with juice,
For every wave brings silly spruces.

Whispering Palms in a Velvet Breeze

Under the palms, the whispers flow,
With secrets shared, the breezes know.
A crab with shades announces the game,
While a parrot caws, 'Isn't this lame?'

The sand makes castles that giggle and sway,
While the sun takes a break, it's winking away.
Laughter bubbles up from the sea,
As fish tell tales of you and me.

A sea cucumber says, 'I'm quite the snack!'
While dolphins joke, 'We'll never look back!'
The stars all wink, pulling pranks on the tide,
As seagulls gather, it's fun they can't hide.

So let's spin around in this oceanic glee,
And dance with the crabs, all wild and free.
With giggles and echoes, the night will unfold,
In joyous whispers, our stories retold.

Star-Dusted Shores Under a Mango Sky

On shores where the waves wear sparkles bright,
We chase after dreams in the warm moonlight.
A mango rolls free, it slips from a hand,
While the sand tickles toes, it's quite unplanned.

The jellyfish bob, wearing hats full of fun,
They jive to the rhythm of a beat from the sun.
A hermit crab holds a contest of speed,
While all the starfish applaud with such greed.

Night's painted in hues of laughter and cheer,
As the ocean sings songs we all long to hear.
A beach ball tumbles, it giggles along,
While the shells join in with a choral song.

The shimmer of joy lights each little face,
As we dance with delight in this magical place.
With hearts all aglow, we surf through the night,
And toast to the fun 'neath the stars shining bright.

Luminous Reflections on Coral Dreams

In waters of azure, the fish crack smiles,
With comical poses that stretch for miles.
Coral reefs sway, dressed up for a ball,
As sea cucumbers waddle and sprawl.

A starfish claims, 'I'm the best-dressed today!'
While seahorses giggle and swim in ballet.
The crabs have a party, they dance in a line,
Dressed to the nines, they drink coconut wine.

The moonlight reflects on their bubbly delight,
With laughter that ripples across the night.
A dolphin strikes poses, it can't stop the show,
While echoing bubbles simply can't slow.

So come join the fun where the ocean gleams,
And share in the laughter of coral dreams.
With each wave that crashes, a new prank begins,
In this world of fun, let the laughter never thin.

Embracing the Night with Painted Skies

The moon wears shades of lemon pie,
While clouds in fancy dresses fly.
Crabs hold parties, dancing crass,
As fish flip flops for the class.

Coconuts roll, they laugh and cheer,
A parrot steals a piña, oh dear!
With waves that tickle sandy toes,
The night chuckles in its prose.

Starfish with goggles glance around,
While jellyfish waltz, they can't be found.
Laughter erupts from turtle towers,
As the night blooms with silly powers.

As laughter fades into the dawn,
The ocean yawns, a sleepy yawn.
Colors splash the horizon bright,
The silly seas bid us goodnight.

Dreams Adrift in the Ocean's Caress.

Beneath the stars, a fish sings low,
While seaweed sways to a comical flow.
A mermaid juggles shells and glee,
Making waves, just wait and see.

Crabs wear hats, they strut with flair,
While dolphins laugh, flipping through air.
The breeze carries jokes from inside shells,
Whispers of antics, oh can you tell?

A walrus slips, oh what a sight,
Surfing on waves, full of delight.
Seagulls squawk in a nonsense chat,
As nightly mischief finds its mat.

But soon the stars begin to fade,
With silly smiles, the night's parade.
As dreams drift back to the ocean's nest,
Tropical giggles find their rest.

Whispers of the Ocean Breeze

The breeze tells tales of silly fish,
Who wish to learn the art of swish.
Crabs wearing glasses, oh so wise,
Misread the tide, but claim a prize.

Seashells gossip with little larks,
While dolphins scribble in the dark.
Waves high-five the shores, they swear,
As marlins swim with less a care.

Starfish paint their toes in pink,
While octopuses sip, and think.
A sea cucumber plays in disguise,
Mischief rolls with ocean tides.

As laughter melds with misty air,
The night wears jokes without a care.
Whispers hug the sandy beach,
Where humor finds its distant reach.

Celestial Dances Under Starry Canopies

Under the glitter of a milky scheme,
A crab competes in a dance-off dream.
The stars blink down, a twinkly cheer,
As conches play tunes for all to hear.

A plucky parrot impersonates a seal,
While sea turtles join in the silly reel.
With glittering shells that spin and glide,
The night becomes a joyous ride.

Guitars strum sweetly up above,
While clams sing songs, and laughter shoves.
Under the canopy of fun-filled sights,
Creatures whirl in carefree flights.

As dawn tiptoes, the party ends,
With belly laughs among ocean friends.
The sky turns bright, a new day's flight,
Yet echoes of fun linger in the light.

Twilight Hues Paint the Island's Dreams

The sun dips low, a golden art,
Palm trees sway, a dance to start.
Laughter rings from near and far,
As island critters join the bazaar.

The sky dons pink, with hints of blue,
A coconut falls, just missed your shoe!
Seagulls squawk their evening song,
While one steals fries, didn't take long!

In the twilight's gentle glow,
Grinning crab plays, putting on a show.
A tourist slips on sandy trails,
While catching scents of sweet cocktails.

The world's a stage, come join the fun,
With each sunset, the night's begun.
In that magic, don't lose your hat,
For the mongoose might just steal that mat!

Waves Cradle the Night's Embrace

The ocean whispers with frothy cheer,
Tickling toes of those drawn near.
A beach ball flies, a seagull dives,
Grandma yells, "Watch out for those jives!"

The water sparkles like sequined gowns,
As kids dodge waves in glowing crowns.
A crab with swagger, struts with pride,
While Dad trips over, gets dragged inside.

Stars twinkle down, a disco flare,
While fish tease the dive and stare.
A splash contest starts, who'll take the crown?
But wait! There goes Mom's fancy gown!

Sandcastles rise, then tumble down,
As laughter echoes all around.
The ocean's playful, a mischievous tease,
With giggles washing on the breeze!

Festivities of the Stars Above

The night awakens with a funky beat,
A conch shell sings, all gather 'round, meet!
The party starts with a limbo stick,
While aunties dance, oh so quick!

Lanterns sway, a cheeky light,
As fireflies join in the fun tonight.
A chubby raccoon disco-dances too,
Stealing snacks and drinks, just for you!

Tomatoes fly in a fruit fight spree,
As laughter bursts like waves at sea.
On island nights, surprise awaits,
A wild adventure; no one hesitates!

Beneath the stars, weird shapes form,
We toast to mishaps, a true island charm.
The moon joins in, a laughing friend,
As the night rolls on, no need to pretend!

The Language of Leaves in the Night

Leaves chuckle softly in midnight's breeze,
As night critters plot, with such ease.
A parrot squawks a joke so sly,
While sneakily, guavas start to fly.

In the shadows, whispers weave,
Creatures gather, their pranks to conceive.
A cheeky mongoose steals a shoe,
While frogs sing ballads just for you!

The moonlight glances through swaying fronds,
Dancing leaves play tricks, like magic wands.
A sloth falls down, unravels the scene,
With giggles rising, it's quite obscene!

So listen closely, hear the night's cheer,
For laughter flows, not a hint of fear.
On this fine eve, nature's delight,
Brings joy in the dark, under the starlight!

Moonlit Waves and Dreaming Palms

Under stars that giggle bright,
The waves dance with pure delight.
Coconuts roll, a cheeky sight,
While seagulls squawk in formal flight.

In flip-flops worn, I take my stand,
Chasing crabs that scurry, unplanned.
A tidal wave of laughter, grand,
As I trip on the soft, warm sand.

The breeze pulls pranks, my hair goes wild,
I try to pose, yet look like a child.
Palm trees sway, so carefree and mild,
Nature's jest, I'm beguiled.

Moonbeams giggle, tickle the sea,
I dance like no one's watching me!
But my shadow trips on a banana tree,
And oh, the night's a comic spree!

Serenade of the Midnight Tide

Whispers of the ocean swell,
Dance with creatures in their shell.
Starfish giggle, oh what a spell,
As jellyfish glide on waves, oh well!

With ukuleles strumming slow,
A crab's debut; stealing the show.
"Clap your claws!" the crowd will crow,
But he waves back, lost in the flow.

Seashells chime in the salty air,
While someone trips, oh what a scare!
Caught in laughter, we all share,
This midnight tide, a wild affair.

The moon's bright grin, a playful sight,
Each splash and giggle makes it right.
Dancing shadows, full of light,
What a funny, glowing night!

Lanterns of the Paradise Sky

With lanterns glowing, bugs in flight,
A ruckus stirs in the balmy night.
The island laughs, a silly sprite,
As drinks spill over, what a sight!

Chillin' lizards, tails entwined,
Stole my snack, oh how unkind!
Meanwhile, I search for my lost mind,
Under stars my thoughts are lined.

The palm fronds sway with a cheerful tune,
While frogs croak praises to the moon.
I joined their song, a wild buffoon,
Frogs took off, I'm left marooned!

With a coconut hat, I crown my face,
As fellow pals join in the race.
We stumble through this merry space,
In giggles and chaos, we find our place.

Echoes of Nightfall on Sandy Shores

Echoes linger, a comical hum,
As crabs and I share an awkward drum.
Sand's in my shoe, with each goofy thrum,
Under moonlight, we're all quite numb.

The tide calls out with a playful roar,
Leaving treasures, oh what a score!
But my beach ball flies out to shore,
While I chase laughter, imploring more.

Drunken palm trees sway and spin,
As seagulls watch with a cheeky grin.
Belly flops from friends, oh let's begin,
These sandy shores, invite the din.

As night falls down with a feathered kiss,
Every mishap turns to bliss.
Comic echoes we can't dismiss,
On sandy shores, we find our bliss!

Breeze-Kissed Melodies of the Night

The palm trees dance, they wiggle and sway,
While crabs in tuxedos come out to play.
Coconuts laugh, throwing shade on the beach,
With the moon as their stage, it's quite the reach.

A parrot tells jokes from a branch high above,
As fish form a band, it's a night full of love.
The waves join in chorus, they splash with delight,
While the fireflies twinkle, keeping spirits bright.

Laughter erupts from a sandcastle throne,
Where clams hold a court, in their shells made of stone.
The breeze tells a secret, a tickle of fun,
While all the night creatures dance under the sun.

So here we shall revel, till dawn breaks our cheer,
With funny old stories, we all want to hear.
As the last of the lanterns burn out on the bay,
Let's giggle till morning, and wish it to stay.

A Symphony of Stars Above the Lagoon

A crab in a top hat conducts from the sand,
He waves his claws, making music so grand.
The fish start to swim, keeping time with the beat,
As the night air fills up with a funky retreat.

Stars twinkle wildly, they're part of the crew,
The moon strums the chords, and the waves hum along too.
With laughter of dolphins, it's quite the parade,
As jellyfish jiggle, in rhythm displayed.

Bubbles burst forth like confetti in flight,
While iguanas sway, in the soft pale moonlight.
It's a concert of creatures, all having a ball,
While the palm fronds applaud, what a night for us all!

And when morning tiptoes with yawns in the glow,
The sea will keep secrets of laughter below.
With echoes of giggles stitched into the breeze,
We'll remember the night, with mischievous ease.

Velvet Skies Touched by Dawn's Glow

As the dawn peeks out with a wink and a grin,
The roosters all chuckle, 'let the fun begin!'
The flamingos are posing, striking a pose,
While the sun does a tango, in the sky's pinky rose.

Dewdrops drop jokes with a splash on the grass,
While iguanas nod and say, 'What a class!'
The waves keep on rolling, with a snickering sound,
As the morning unfolds, giggles come round.

The clouds like fluffy marshmallows float by,
While gulls play charades, drawing laughs from the sky.
A parrot drops puns with a chirpy refrain,
As the world wakes to laughter, like sunshine with rain.

So let us all bask in this bright, playful cheer,
With whispers of night still echoing near.
For each dawn is a promise, of mischief and fun,
In the land of the lizards, where laughter's never done.

Romance Beneath the Canopy of Dreams

In a hammock made of laughter, swaying so free,
Two lovebirds giggle, sipping sweet tea.
With fireflies winking like stars in a row,
It's a dance of romance with a twist of a show.

The palm leaves gossip, sharing tales from the past,
While lovers exchange glances, and moments amassed.
The frogs croak a tune, serenading the night,
As the moon sneaks a listen, casting soft light.

With coconuts chatting about love in the air,
And the breeze plays matchmaker — oh, such a flair!
A cute little crab delivers love notes,
While the sand beneath tickles, and joy gently floats.

So here in this paradise, laughter takes flight,
Beneath leafy secrets and stars shining bright.
With each playful glance, and a twinkle of mirth,
Our hearts say, 'This joy is the best on Earth!'

Reflections in the Velvet Waters

The moon's a big pizza in the sky,
Splashing cheese on waves passing by.
Fish are dancing, shaking their tails,
While turtles try to squeak out some scales.

A coconut floats, it thinks it's a boat,
An octopus laughs, and starts to gloat.
Crabs join the party, on tiny chairs,
Waving their claws, without any cares.

Starfish sing karaoke, quite out of tune,
A pufferfish joins, making all swoon.
The seaweed sways, in a hilarious twist,
As dolphins jump in an all-night tryst.

With laughter and bubbles, the night takes flight,
In this lagoon of mirth, everything feels right.
To toast with a shell, raise your drink of salt,
Let's dance in the bubbles, it's nobody's fault!

Midnight Blossom of the Tropics

A flower blooms, with a giggle and wink,
It talks to a butterfly, gives it a drink.
The petals all blush, in a colorful cheer,
As crickets provide the soundtrack we hear.

Bananas get silly, with laughter they swing,
While mangoes roll over, and start to sing.
The night air is spicy, with humor and zest,
Who knew tropical blooms could laugh with the best?

A little frog hops, in a top hat so grand,
He's dancing with lizards, their moves all unplanned.
The night's like a party, where all are invited,
With jokes in the breeze, no one feels slighted.

As moonbeams join in, with a playful smirk,
The garden erupts, in a cheerful quirk.
Let's sway with the petals, and dance through the night,
With flowers and friends, everything feels right!

Secrets Sway in the Palm Shadows

The palms are in whispers, spinning a yarn,
About the wild monkey that stole a barn.
A parrot chimes in with a joke about fruit,
While iguanas watch with a laugh that's quite cute.

The shadows create a secretive dance,
As crabs make quick moves, in a grand game of chance.
A breeze tells a story, of one silly fish,
Who swam with a dolphin, and made quite the splash!

A sandcastle rallies, with dreams of a throne,
While starfish hold court, the king feels at home.
With seashells debating, and seagulls that jest,
The night holds its breath for the funniest quest.

From the swaying palms, a giggle slips free,
Underneath the bright stars, all feel so carefree.
So gather your friends, let the laughter ignite,
In this playful palette, everything feels right!

Glistening Pearls Beneath the Moon

The oysters are laughing, they're ticklish inside,
As pearls roll about, on a wonderful ride.
A clam tells a pun, so cheesy and bright,
While jellyfish giggle, floating through light.

Beneath the soft glow, sea cucumbers sway,
With starfish cheering for the pearls on display.
A dolphin does tricks, with a splash and a spin,
As fishy friends gather, to see who will win.

Corals are painting, with hues of delight,
Drawing smiles on the jelly, a magnificent sight.
Anemones wave, like they're leading a band,
Inviting the sea to join in their stand.

With laughter and sparkles, the ocean's aglow,
In this wacky wonderland, let your joy flow.
So dive into fun, as the tides do align,
For pearls beneath waves hold the laughter divine!

Luminous Secrets Amidst Coconut Trees

Coconuts giggle in the moonlight,
Swaying gently, a funny sight.
Chickens wear shades, strutting so proud,
Beneath the palms, they dance like a crowd.

The crabs throw parties with the tide,
In little hats, they scuttle and glide.
Starfish gossip, their voices are hushed,
As the seaweed wigs get fabulously brushed.

The breeze delivers jokes from afar,
While the fireflies practice their guitar.
Even the waves join in with a roar,
Tickling the shores, they beg for encore.

Under the stars, our laughter cascades,
In this bizarre realm, the silliness invades.
Life's a comedy, we all take our roles,
Dancing with nature, our goofy souls.

Rhythm of the Island Night

The conch shells blow a tune so sweet,
Dancing feet follow the rhythmic beat.
Lobsters in tuxedos, what a delight,
Join the parade under starlit night.

A toucan sings with a wobbly tone,
While a wild boar tries to dance alone.
Palm fronds wave like they're losing their mind,
As the island grooves, it's one of a kind.

Even the moon cracks a cheeky grin,
As the party rolls on, let the fun begin.
Fireworks in the ocean, a sparkling sight,
While the dolphins giggle, bouncing in flight.

With laughter and joy, the night unfolds,
As mischief and merriment silently molds.
In this magical hour, we lose all our cares,
Caught in the rhythm, all worries wear snares.

Dreams Woven in the Coral Breeze

In the coral gardens, mischief brews,
Octopuses wear party hats and shoes.
Little fish swim in a synchronized line,
Their tiny disco, oh so divine.

Jellyfish bounce on invisible beats,
Tickling the turtles with their soft fleets.
While a seahorse juggles shells in a show,
The clownfish chuckle, "Hey, look at that flow!"

With every wave, a story unfolds,
The laughter of fishes, the secrets it holds.
Mermaids giggle, their laughter so light,
Dreams intertwine in the coral's delight.

As night falls softly, the stars take flight,
Our giggles entwined, wrapped tight in the night.
In this whimsical world, we frolic with ease,
Searching for joy in the coral breeze.

Dance of the Fireflies at Dusk

Fireflies flicker like tiny lamps,
Creating a dance that brightens the camps.
They twirl and swerve, with no cares to share,
Even the frogs jump in for a flair.

In the jungle, a party brews strong,
As the monkeys sing off-key all night long.
While the lizards strut in sequined attire,
The audience laughs, their joy won't tire.

Bananas wear hats and giggle with glee,
Celebrating life, wild and free.
Beneath the stars, in this playful land,
Every creature joins in, hand-in-hand.

A chorus of chuckles fills the air,
As the night sparkles with whimsical flair.
Together we dance, with light in our hearts,
In this dazzling world, where the laughter starts.

Echoes of Laughter Beneath Palm Canopies

Underneath the swaying trees,
The crabs are throwing wild parties,
With coconuts as their drinks,
And seagulls serving snacks, oh the antics!

Jellyfish play tag in the dark,
While the starfish steal the spotlight,
One clam forgot his dance moves,
But he still shuffles with all his might!

The tides roll in to the beat,
Crickets chirp a melody sweet,
Even the waves can't help but giggle,
As they crash and do their little wiggle.

By sunrise, the laughter takes flight,
As the birds now join the delight,
The ocean's grin is a sight to behold,
In this paradise, life's never old!

Silken Sands and Firefly Serenades

The fireflies sparkle like jokes in the air,
While sandcastles wobble without a care,
A crab with a top hat struts by with flair,
    Sands tickle toes, beg for a dare!

Seashells gossip, they've got stories to share,
    Of snails in high fashion, quite rare,
    Laughter fills the breezes with zest,
As we dance with the stars, feeling blessed!

Footprints tell tales of a night full of glee,
Where the ocean fished for a tune, you see,
We twirled around and lost track of time,
    Only to find we're all in our prime!

And when the sun spills gold on the sand,
    The fun never ends, it's all so grand,
With giggles resounding, joy takes the lead,
This night in paradise plants a smile, indeed!

Midnight Blooms and Ocean Whispers

In gardens where they can giggle and yawn,
Flowers tease the moon with a daffodil scorn,
The breeze tells jokes that make the waves roar,
As dolphins join in with a splashy encore!

Butterflies whisper secrets so sly,
While petals play hide-and-seek in the sky,
A crab tried stand-up, but fell on his shell,
Yet laughter erupts like a bubbling swell!

The night wraps us with quilts starry and bright,
As the fireflies boogie in a dazzling flight,
Seashells giggle at every twist and turn,
For this circus of nature, we all gladly yearn!

With the ocean's embrace, and laughter so free,
Who knew the night could be such glee?
Beneath the blooms, joy takes its stance,
In this whimsical wonder, we all find our dance!

Lustrous Horizons Where Waves Kiss the Stars

Waves tickle toes with frothy delight,
While crabs wear sunglasses, taking the night,
Moonbeams cast light on a ship's quirky crew,
As they dance on deck, too cool for the view!

The stars play poker with comets in tow,
With the ocean as dealer, putting on a show,
Seashells gather round for popcorn and cheer,
Waving their arms, it's the best night of the year!

The wind tells tales of mermaids that sing,
As the tides march forth, a slapstick fling,
Laughter bounces up from sea to the sky,
In this festive realm, let your troubles fly!

As dawn draws close, the giggles don't cease,
For every wave carries a grain of peace,
With joy in our hearts and fun on the way,
We'll savor these nights, come what may!

Reflecting Waves and Glittering Stars

The ocean's doing the waltz, you see,
With fishy friends in flappy glee.
A crab in a tux, he struts with pride,
While seaweed dances, like it's bonafide.

Starfish are lounging, sipping on tea,
Complaining about how their arms can't flee.
Manta rays gossip, flipping their fins,
While turtles nod off, dreaming of spins.

A jellyfish giggles, it's quite a sight,
Bobbing along in the moon's soft light.
The seagulls caw jokes that make you snort,
As dolphins prank call, thinking it's sport.

So raise a toast to the night's silly cheer,
With sand between toes, and nothing to fear.
The waves will keep laughing, 'til morning's glare,
In this underwater comedy, full of flair.

Secrets of the Night Wrapped in Orchids

Under velvet skies where secrets bloom,
Orchids in gowns dance to the moon.
A coconut laughs, all full of cheer,
While parrots swap jokes, ear to ear.

The breeze whispers tales of fantastic beasts,
With a sloth who's rapping at midnight feasts.
Monkeys perform in a foliage show,
Swinging through branches, putting on a glow.

In the shadows, a gecko takes flight,
Chasing those dreams in the tropical night.
A frog on a leaf, he croaks out a tune,
While fireflies dance in a wild cartoon.

So hang up your worries, take a wild chance,
And mingle with critters, join in the dance.
The secrets of night, they giggle and sway,
With flowers as witnesses to this cabaret.

Gentle Currents of Evening's Embrace

The currents bubble with playful delight,
As fish tell fish tales, oh what a sight!
An eel in his tux shares a royal jest,
While clams try to beat him, but fail the test.

Moonbeams tickle the waves with a grin,
While a lionfish struts, with sequins to spin.
Octopuses whirl, practicing their dance,
In an underwater disco, it's quite the chance!

A starfish stands up, declaring a vote,
For best-dressed creature in a fancy coat.
The winner's a sea cucumber, can you believe?
With a leafy crown, making schemes up his sleeve.

As the tide rolls in, the laughter won't fade,
Undercover shenanigans are skillfully played.
Join in the merriment, don't be afraid,
In the gentle embrace where wonders parade.

Solstice Serenade Under the Night's Veil

When the sun dips low and the stars align,
Crickets start crooning, their tunes divine.
A stargazer turtle wears shades with flair,
   Sipping on seafoam, without a care.

Fireflies gather for a whimsical plot,
In a glow worm tailgate, oh what a lot!
Beetles roll dice, in the sands they bet,
While a wise old crab plays the violin set.

Palm trees sway, trying to join the fun,
With coconut drinks, they shine like the sun.
And somewhere a parrot is stealing the show,
   With jokes that land just like a pro.

So dance with the shadows, let laughter unfurl,
In this night's fairy tale, let dreams take a whirl.
With moonbeams as spotlights, the magic is real,
In this solstice serenade, come share the appeal.

Dance of the Bioluminescent Tide

The waves have a glow like a disco ball,
Fish in their tuxedos come to the call.
Dancing with jellyfish under the moon,
Who knew sea creatures could bust a tune?

Crabs do the cha-cha, all sideways and spry,
While seaweed does limbo, oh my, oh my!
A starfish attempts a funky new move,
But ends up just sitting, in the groove.

Manta rays glide with a boisterous flair,
As mermaids drop hints about matching their hair.
The ocean's a party, so bring your best jest,
Join in the fun, it's a watery fest!

So if you swim by where the sea creatures twine,
You'll see quite the show, it's just divine!
Laugh as they shimmy and wiggle with glee,
Dance with the tide—it's the place to be!

Tropical Sighs in a Midnight Garden

In the garden where flowers have secrets to share,
A sloth on a branch flips its hair without care.
Cacti throw shade, while the palms giggle loud,
As moonbeams join in, like they're part of the crowd.

A parrot named Pierre thinks he's quite suave,
Telling tall tales to a group of young braves.
"Once I flew high, through clouds made of cream,
And I slipped on a cherry, oh, what a dream!"

Fireflies wear glasses, looking clever and bright,
While crickets play chess, in the cool of the night.
Flora's become a stand-up comedian's show,
Laughter erupts, as the fruit flies all flow.

In this enchanted jungle, pure joy meets surprise,
Each moment unfolds, under starlit skies.
So, raise your gin and tonic with zest,
And toast to the garden, it's truly the best!

Chasing Shadows on Sun-Kissed Paths

On sun-kissed paths where the shadows play,
A monkey's on a skateboard, rolling away.
Squirrels critique his daring new ride,
While butterflies giggle and choose sides.

To chase down the shadows, a snail bows down low,
With determination, it's ready to go!
But alas, it stops for a snack on the way,
"I'll catch those shadows, just after this hay."

Luau in the distance, laughter in waves,
Where fruitcakes dance, and the pineapple raves.
Watermelons jive like they're busting a groove,
Each slice tells a story, together they move.

So, join in the chase, there's no time to waste,
With giggles and grins sharing joyful haste.
Some shadows may run, but we'll have the last laugh,
In this wacky parade down the sun-kissed path!

Serene Melodies of the Nightingale's Call

The nightingale sings with a flair so warm,
Even the owls raise a brow at its charm.
"Is that a songbird or a jazz saxophonist?
Sounds like a party we absolutely missed!"

The frogs join in, croaking harmonies loud,
Making a chorus that's one crazy crowd.
Crickets refuse to be outshined, you see,
They bring the beat, while the fireflies flee.

A turtle with glasses narrates the night,
"Back in my day, we were cooler, that's right!
We'd breakdance on lily pads, hip and sublime,
Now we just sit, and wait for the time!"

With chuckles and chirps, melodies entwine,
As moonlight cascades, everything's fine.
In this comedic symphony under stars bright,
We laugh at the tunes, in this whimsical night!

The Silent Chime of a Night's Lullaby

In the stillness, crabs dance cheeky,
Waves whisper secrets, oh so sneaky.
A coconut drops with a thud and a plop,
As the moon laughs, it just won't stop.

Chasing fireflies, I trip on my shoe,
While palm trees giggle; they know what to do.
A parrot squawks jokes, perched high in the dark,
And a dolphin winks, plays the night like a lark.

Shells giggle softly, tucked in the sand,
Together they gossip, they form a band.
Stars twinkle so bright, but they look quite daft,
As they pick up the beat of the ocean's craft.

So let's dance on the shore, where the sand's warm and nice,
With the tide's silly rhythm, we won't think twice.
Who needs beauty sleep when the night is so zany?
Let's laugh with the sea, it's all kind of grainy!

Where the Sapphire Sea Meets the Sky

The horizon teases with a wink and a grin,
Clouds wear sunglasses, let the fun begin.
Seagulls squawk tunes that are just so absurd,
While a crab sings ballads, but I can't hear the words.

Bubbles from cocktails float right by the shore,
They pop with a giggle, and then want some more.
Fish swim in circles, wearing tiny top hats,
They throw a big party; all their friends are the cats.

Laughter erupts as we dive for the waves,
Each splash sends a message; the ocean behaves.
It tickles our toes like a playful breeze,
While conch shells chime in like a band of sweet bees.

So raise your glass high, let's toast to this night,
With joy in our hearts and the stars in our sight.
The sapphire sea sparkles, but it's hard to discern,
If it's magic or mischief, we'll let the tide turn!

Nocturne of the Coral Jewels

Underwater whispers, a clam tells a tale,
Of octopuses dancing, they never seem pale.
The coral polka dots, they jiggle in time,
While a shrimp cracks jokes, with a pinch of lime.

Drifting through anemones, the sea fans sway,
As turtles tell stories of the good old days.
A starfish drops puns, with arms all around,
And a playful sea horse just twirls underground.

Market stalls bob from the waves to the sun,
Selling jokes like fresh fish, all just for fun.
A parrotfish carols, with glittering hues,
While we laugh and shake, in our party shoes.

So come take a dip in this kingdom so bright,
Where the jewels of the ocean shine days and nights.
Let the laughter echo, as the waves play along,
It's a nocturne of joy, where we all belong!

Warm Tides and Gentle Rays

The sun takes a break, bids the day adieu,
While sandcastles giggle, as the night feels new.
Shadows play tag with the palm trees around,
And a loose beachball rolls, making a sound.

Drinks in coconuts, they smile like friends,
With umbrellas poking out, they set the trends.
A hermit crab giggles, in its borrowed shell,
As it sidesteps the currents, it dances so well.

The stars drop their sequins, just like confetti,
While the waves hum a tune, airy and petty.
The moon pulls the tide, in a comforting hug,
While the sea whispers secrets, soft as a shrug.

So let's relish the humor in this sandy delight,
As laughter and warmth fill the magical night.
With each wave that crashes and each smile we wear,
We'll be silly forever, in this laughter we share!

Mystical Dreams in a Land of Palms

Underneath the swaying trees,
Coconuts fall with a soft wheeze.
I dream of snorkeling with a fish,
Who whispers secrets of my wish.

The crabs all dance in pairs, you see,
Wearing tiny hats, oh so fancy!
A parrot squawks, 'Join the parade!'
While tourists laugh and lemonade's made.

Bikinis and shorts, a colorful sight,
Getting sunburned is quite a fright!
But every giggle makes it alright,
In these mystical dreams of pure delight.

So bring your floaties, party hats too,
For a night of madness under the moon's hue!
We'll toast to dreams, and maybe a shark,
As we dance till dawn, igniting the spark.

Starlit Whispers and Ocean's Breath

In the moonlight, the waves begin to rhyme,
A dolphin flips, oh isn't that sublime?
The beach is buzzing with laughter and cheer,
While sand castles wobble as kids draw near.

The stars wink down like mischievous elves,
While seashells giggle, talking to themselves.
A crab on a mission, with a colorful hat,
Trying to impress a nearby chatty cat.

The tide comes in, now look at those folks!
They're running and squealing, those silly blokes!
Splashing about in the foamy glow,
Chasing the waves, stealing the show.

Oh listen closely to the ocean's song,
It's full of giggles that can't be wrong.
With a twist and a turn, we sway and glide,
In this starlit wonder, all fun and pride.

Dance of the Fireflies at Dusk

Tiny lights twinkle in the evening sky,
Fireflies zoom, as if to fly high.
With jars in hand, kids race around,
Giggling triumphs in the grass they found.

A luau begins with tacos on the grill,
While everyone laughs, their hearts to fill.
An uncle attempts a hula with flair,
Tripping over his feet, laughter fills the air.

The rhythm of night, a festive show,
As the coconut water starts to flow.
Dance like no one's watching, and if they do,
You'll leave them chuckling, in this funny view.

So come, join the dance, make memories bright,
With fireflies twinkling, let's party all night!
With laughter we'll sway, under stars so wide,
In this magical hush, let joy be our guide.

Rhythms of a Warm Island Breeze

The palm trees sway to a funny beat,
While seagulls squawk in their goofy greet.
A smoothie spills on a sunburned toe,
And suddenly, laughter starts to flow.

Sandy toes and shades tossed to the side,
Chasing each other, full of island pride.
A limbo contest, let's see who can bend,
While clumsy tourists make quite the trend.

The sun starts to set, embracing the night,
With fruit platters bursting in vibrant light.
A conch shell's blow brings a giggling crowd,
As a cat naps nearby, snoring out loud.

So gather your friends and let's make a scene,
With rhythms of laughter, joyful and keen.
Here's to the fun, and a toast to the breeze,
In this warm, silly paradise, let's do as we please.

Twilight Tales of the Sapphire Sea

Beneath the stars, a crab in shades,
Dances a jig in conch shell parades.
Fish throw a party, all with a splash,
While seahorses gossip, oh what a clash!

A shark brings a cake, it's three tiers tall,
But oops! A dolphin swims, causing a sprawl.
With a flick and a flop, the cake drops down,
Underwater laughter fills the whole town!

The octopus plays, wearing a hat,
Juggling clams while the turtles chat.
A glimmer of scales, what a sight to see,
A dance-off ensues, oh, it's quite the spree!

As the night unfolds with laughter so bright,
Just know, the ocean's got party vibes right!
Under the moon, we'll twirl and spin,
In this coastal affair, everyone wins!

Haunting Harmonies of Night's Embrace

In the jungle depths, a monkey sings,
While chasing fireflies on invisible strings.
Parrots squawk jokes that make us all giggle,
As we swat at mosquitoes—what a fine riddle!

A raccoon joins in with a tap and a twist,
He's got a fine knack for planning a list.
"Midnight snacks," he claims, "are the best sort!"
While serving us berries, his gourmet resort!

A sloth, oh so slow, tells a ghost tale,
But by the end, he's forgotten the trail!
With yawns and sleepy eyes, we hear him say,
"Let's haunt the fridge in a spooky ballet!"

Together we chuckle beneath the moon's glow,
In our vibrant forest, where the antics flow.
With whispers and howls, and laughter we make,
In this wild serenade, we never awake!

Soaked in Moonlight and Tidal Echoes

On the beach, the waves sing a tune,
As crabs line dance under a bright balloon.
Seagulls strut by with a fashionable flair,
While a turtle does yoga—oh, what a pair!

A pelican drops in with his soggy shoes,
Sipping on coconuts with nothing to lose.
He's solved all the problems that come in a wave,
While sharing his wisdom—so bold, so brave!

The starfish play poker, an odd little game,
With shells as their chips—oh, who's really to blame?
The otters bring snacks, karaoke begins,
And even the clams join—no one ever wins!

As the night splashes joy, we dance and we sway,
In this salty paradise, we laugh, come what may.
With echoes of fun in the cool ocean breeze,
We'll bottle these moments like summer's sweet tease!

Lush Gardens Under a Silvery Canopy

In the garden, a frog croaks the news,
Wearing bright boots and too many hues.
A lizard does flips while sipping on tea,
While the roses are gossiping, "Can you believe?"

With blooms sharing secrets, it's hard to keep track,
The daisies laugh loudly, 'We'll never look back!'
The sunflower spins, spins, spins with delight,
As fireflies twinkle in the cool, sweet night!

A hedgehog, quite shy, has a pun or two,
That sends all the petals into a big hue.
The bees gather round, buzzing just for the show,
While munching on petals, they dance to and fro!

As the moon grins down, casting light all around,
In this garden of giggles, pure joy can be found.
With friends all around, laughter floats in the air,
In this whimsical place, there's always a flare!

Ukulele Serenade on a Starlit Beach

Under the moon, the ukulele strums,
Crabs dance around, to the beat they come.
The seagulls laugh, on a quest for some fries,
As my drink tips over, oh what a surprise!

Palm trees sway, in a hula-like trance,
A squirrel with shades tries to join in the dance.
Shells giggle softly, all quiet and sly,
Watching the antics, as time drifts by.

The sand is a carpet for party shoes worn,
While beach balls bounce, like a kid just reborn.
Pineapple hats bounce, oh what a sight,
In this crazy place, everything feels right!

We toast to the night, with coconuts in hand,
As fish in tuxedos, start a conga band.
So here on this shore, with laughter and cheer,
Every sunset's magic, the night's drawing near!

When the Coconut Fronds Sing

Coconuts gossip, in rustling delight,
Whispering secrets till late in the night.
They say the moon stole their favorite dress,
While crabs in tuxedos just want to impress!

The ocean hums softly, a tune that we share,
While pineapples giggle, 'Man, how can we care?'
A parrot in shades, calls the crowd with a squawk,
As everything dances, even the rock!

Stars trade their stories, in glittery threads,
As dolphins come swim, with crowns on their heads.
They challenge the waves, for the biggest splash,
While sea turtles dive slow, becoming quite brash.

Under the palms, we feast on the night,
With nachos that jump, and smoothies in flight.
This tropical chaos is where we all cling,
Laughter in the air, when the fronds start to sing!

The Enchanted Hour of Silver Waves

In the hour of magic, the waves do a dance,
With jellyfish twirls, they entrance in a glance.
A crab on a surfboard, with all of its flair,
Sips a smoothie while taking mid-air!

The moon is a lifeguard, watching our glee,
As the fish in tuxedos swim by with a spree.
A coconut blows whistles from high in the skies,
While seaweed waltzes, to laughter's surprise.

Tropical breezes weave jokes in the air,
Popcorn on fire flies without any care.
The beach is alive, full of giggles and lights,
Where even the stars wink, embracing the nights!

As midnight approaches, we dance on the shore,
With jellybeans falling, who could ask for more?
This enchanted hour, sweet and full of plays,
Marks a night full of joy, in shimmering bays.

Nightscapes Alive with Tropical Whispers

Whispers of fun curl around in the dark,
While lanterns flicker, igniting a spark.
The lizards wear hats, oh they're so refined,
Sipping on mojitos, quite one of a kind!

Stars gossip softly, sharing tales from above,
While sea shells conspire, spreading laughter and love.
A banana peel slips, sending crabs (oh so proud),
Flipping and flopping, falling flat with a crowd!

Playing limbo, the palms bend quite low,
Holding contests in salsa, igniting a show.
Mermaids applaud, as waves offer a cheer,
For the shenanigans found in the atmosphere.

With every nightfall, magic slips into view,
As coconuts chatter, just between us two.
So let's cherish the night, with giggles and lore,
For life in the tropics is never a bore!

www.ingramcontent.com/pod-product-compliance
Lightning Source LLC
Chambersburg PA
CBHW072131070526
44585CB00016B/1623